Writing begins at home

Preparing children for writing before they go to school

Marie Clay

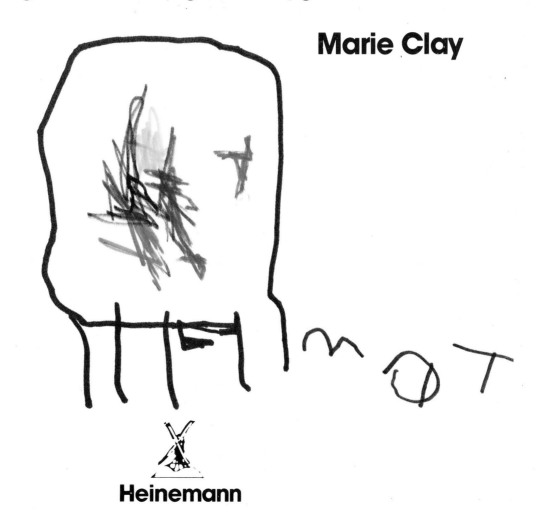

Heinemann

Published by Heinemann Education, a division of Reed Publishing
(NZ) Ltd, 39 Rawene Road, Birkenhead, Auckland. Associated companies,
branches and representatives throughout the world.

ISBN 0 86863 277 5
US ISBN 0 435 08452 6

© 1987 Marie M. Clay

First published 1987,
Reprinted 1992, 1993, 1994, 1996 (Twice)

Printed in Hong Kong

Other books by Marie Clay
Reading: The Patterning of Complex Behaviour
Sand (Concepts About Print Test)
Stones (Concepts About Print Test)
What Did I Write?
Reading Begins at Home (Co-author)
Observing Young Readers
Record of Oral Language and Biks and Gutches
(Co-author)
Becoming Literate
Writing Begins at Home
Observation Survey
Reading Recovery

Contents

1 Getting in touch   4

2 Exploration and discoveries   8

3 'I want to record a message'   19

4 We follow Sally-Ann's progress   22

5 Individual differences at school entry   40

6 How can a parent help?   43

7 The child at school   51

8 Let your child lead   62

1 Getting in touch

Questions from parents

How do children begin writing in its earliest stages?

How do little children find out about written messages?

What do they learn from the people around them?

What do they discover for themselves?

How do preschool children learn to tell the difference between drawing, pictures, numbers and letters, print and cursive writing?

In some homes people teach children about writing and in other homes there are few opportunities for learning to write. Does this make a difference?

This book is about . . .

This is a book about many different preschool children who discovered some of the secrets of printed language and moved a long way towards writing their own stories before they went to school. It is not a book about learning to print. It is not going to tell you how to have a spelling genius who is only three or four years old.

Drawing and dictating

When Delwyn was five and had been at school for two months, her teacher asked her to draw something. She drew a teddy bear. Then she dictated a story:

'My favourite toy is a teddy bear.'

The teacher wrote it down for her.

My favourite toy is a teddy bear.

Delwyn, five years two months

Constructing stories

Writing stories is about ideas and plots and story language ('Once upon a time'), and letters.

Sally-Ann's work shows this. We do not know whether the print, or the pictures, or the idea for the story came first, but she constructed them all. She said, 'Here's a story for you, Dad.'

Once upon a time there was a little girl who went for a walk and she met a tortoise who turned into a balloon . . . . There's a poem there, too, Dad.

Sally-Ann was four and she would go to school in another 12 months.

Sally-Ann, four years

It is fun to observe

Ask a child of two to seven years to write something for you. Don't be trapped into teaching. Stand back and observe closely how the child goes about it. Show some interest and support the child's engagement in the task.

Then ask if you may have the writing to keep. (Usually you will get it but not always when you first ask.)

Not all children show an interest in making marks on paper. In some homes children would never see an adult do this. Older brothers and sisters may do 'homework', though.

Children love to play with a pencil or with coloured pens. For them it is like exploring. New discoveries emerge at almost every encounter. The activity itself brings its own satisfactions. And development seems to have more to do with opportunity to explore print than with intelligence or age. Children of very different ages can be seen doing similar things in preschool writing. There do not seem to be set sequences through which each child must pass.

If you are close to a child in this age group and this development interests you, you might like to keep a folder of samples. You will find that you can capture the changes that occur, and that it is as interesting as your child's photo album. This record can be shown to people like fond grandparents, or kept hidden away for parents to look back on. It helps if you understand a little about the kinds of progress that can be made. The samples in this book try to help you to do that.

No one can be certain about what is happening in a particular child's writing. It is fine to be tentative and unsure. Time and again you will find that what the child does will not be what you expect. You will often need to change your ideas because the child has gone off on another learning track.

It may take two or three years before the child can record 'real' messages in words that you can read, but they will be interesting years.

Tiahomarama, one year six months.
He knew what a pen was for.

A word about materials

The intention to write may be the most important thing that children bring to this learning.

A home that wants to foster writing will organise a space — time — and materials to be available if the child wants to write.

Create some opportunities for writing and pay attention to what the child does.

Pencils, pens, felt pens and crayons — anything that can write will be explored. Old wrapping papers or cardboard scraps are fine to write on. Newspapers and old magazines can be used but the child prefers blank spaces. A preschooler has little need for lined paper. Perhaps you could collect spare papers in a box from which the child could choose. Different colours and sizes seem to attract children.

Think of a mother trying to occupy her child after 30 minutes in the doctor's waiting room. Inside her purse she finds the blank side of the bill she has just paid and the little diary pencil she was given for Christmas. Saved, she sets the child to work, which occupies two minutes, or perhaps five if she is lucky.

Young children's attention is brief at first but this increases as children learn more about the task.

Another approach to materials is for parents to talk about writing as they themselves are doing it, explaining what they are doing. Or they may talk to the child about reading a letter or notice, or sending a greeting card, or paying a bill. Children may want to join in and fill out a bank deposit slip, copy a bus ticket, or send a greeting to Grandma.

Keep samples of your child's attempts to write. You will need a big folder, or a scrapbook, or a ring binder, or an album of see-through pockets used for photos. That way you can have a record of this exciting exploration by the young writer. Always date the sample and write a note of how the writing came about and what the child said about it.

Lauren and her mother shared this letter to Grandma

2 Exploration and discoveries

Exploring with pen or pencil

Most adults call the earliest attempts at writing, scribble.

Often children seem to ask the question 'What can I *do*?' If you watch the child at work it is as if they have said, 'What will happen if I do this or that?'

Ted, at 15 months, and Jamie at two years 10 months, may have been at this stage, acting first, and looking to see what happened.

Spontaneous exploring like this should be what 'writing' is about in the preschool years.

This is a book about opportunities to become a writer. It is not a book about teaching your child to write. A deliberate attempt to teach may succeed, but it also runs the risk of making a child avoid these activities.

Ted, one year three months

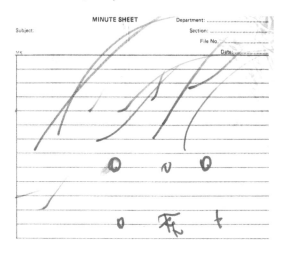

Jamie, two years 10 months

Discovering forms

Scribble takes many forms. Out of those first explorations come some forms that the child can recognise. Often these are circles and the scribble streamers which may be curled or made of zig-zag lines.

Movement and form come together here. Perhaps the child can now anticipate, 'If I do that I will see a circle or a streamer or a line.'

So, exploring movements lead to an expectancy to see certain shapes. Circular motions, lines, and crosses are used most often.

Haromi, two years eight months
He putiputi — a flower

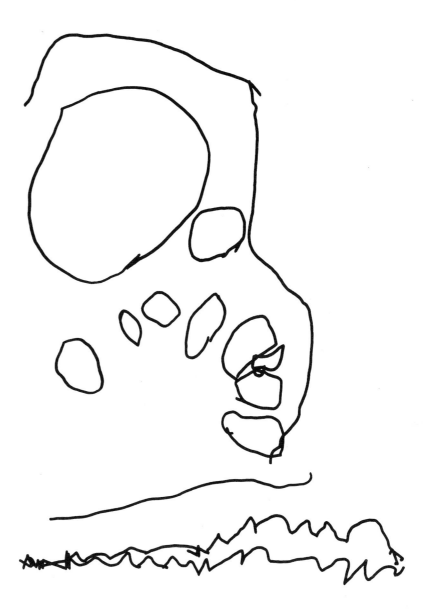

Nicky, three years two months

9

Drawing particular pictures to carry a message

In a limited way the child begins to represent the things he knows in real life or the ones that occur in books. These drawings evolve out of the lines and shapes that have developed as movements were explored.

Manuka's horse, drawn at four years, is quite elaborate. It has three riders on its back.

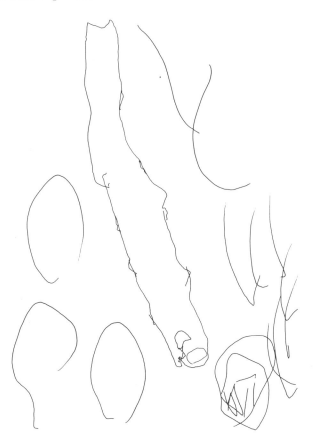

Aaron, aged three, drew 'A big ghost with eyes. It doesn't need a mouth. It doesn't talk.'

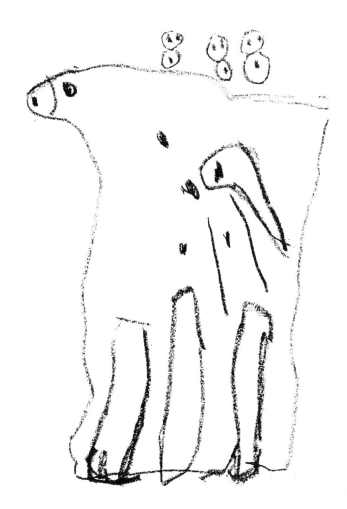

The five-year-old's cows are more informative than you would think. The dictated story was, 'The cows are running around the farm.' The extra bit of information is that one cow has a calf inside her!

My father is taking me to London.

There is a clear intention to put a message across in these pictures. The dictated story confirms this.

Drawing is different from writing

Out of scribble there usually emerges a distinction between writing and drawing. The distinction may be hard for adults to explain. Somehow the preschooler discovers the difference.

Drawing is one thing. Writing is another.

When Mark was three years nine months, and drawing boys in detail, he was asked to write something. His idea of writing had some of the characteristics of single letters.

Mark's younger sister, Denise, was two years seven months and two years nine months when she produced samples which suggest that she already distinguished writing from drawing. A letter 't' had emerged (or was it just a cross?). It was placed first, last and in the middle of the patterns, which is where letters can go. She linked these with scribble streamers.

By three and a half Denise has extended her list of signs slowly to

o t o

with some other variants. Denise had discovered most of this for herself.

Mark, three years nine months
Drawing

Mark, three years nine months
Writing

Change over 14 months

Denise, two years seven months

Three months later she wrote her father's name and extended the statement with a sequence that alternates the 'o' and 't' forms.

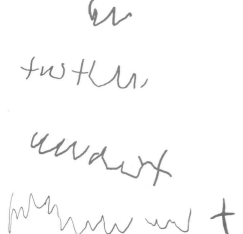

Denise, two years nine months

Denise, three years six months

Denise, three years nine months

13

There are many different ways to start

Children often start with a scribble streamer. It is easy to make and it looks a bit like adult writing.

Sometimes it is written line after line, just as adults write letters to relatives in script writing. In Annie's letter (top right) the place of the message is held by scribble script but in the middle is an almost recognisable word. It is not David. It is

AnniD

When the scribble streamer becomes a line of separate marks the child has gained a new concept. At three years nine months Annie can enter details on the lines of the Savings Bank form. She makes separate signs one after the other with admirable control.

Annie, three years six months

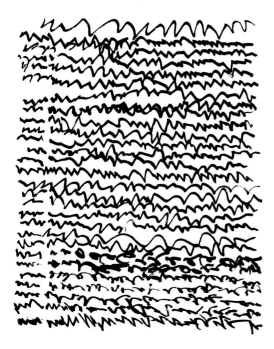

Annie, three years eight months

PARTICULARS OF CHEQUES (to be entered by Depositor)			
CHEQUE ISSUED BY	BANK	BRANCH	AMOUNT
Cheques, etc., included in this deposit cannot be drawn against until proceeds have been collected.	TOTAL $		

Laura, four years six months

Refining the forms

Out of the scribbling, out of the forms, come the repeatable signs.

Laura draws and scribbles (top left). She points to the 'L' she has written and says, 'That's a down and across "L", just like Laura.'

The exploration continues. Bits of signs can be isolated, and recombined, and turned around, and put upside down.

Children explore signs, their position, their variants. How much variety can I make? How much decoration can I add?

Which are print signs? When is a sign not a sign? What are the limits to changing a letter? If you point out that a sign is not a letter because it has too many strokes or curves the young writer is likely to tell you, 'I like to have it that way!' (See Sally-Ann p.23.)

Children's scribbles often start at an early age. On one particular occasion when Sandra was two and a half years she was making marks on paper with great concentration and her mother asked, 'Are you drawing a lovely picture?'

(Full marks to mother for attending to the activity.)

The reply came quickly. 'No, I'm writing a "S" for Sandra.'

15

The traps that adults do not see

There is great confusion ahead of children in the little traps that we adults often do not recognise. We know what we are talking about!

So we go off to the Post Office to mail Nana's letter, or out to the letter box to collect the letters that the postman brought us. Junior sits down with his pencil to make letters. What will he make?

One preschool genius combined both meanings. He drew a page for the letter and then he put mock letters like 't's inside.

A more uncertain five-year-old drew a picture for his teacher. He was a child learning to speak English. When asked what he had drawn, he said, 'A l'dder,' and the teacher wrote 'a ladder' on his drawing. I often wondered if his drawing and naming were some kind of compromise in his mind between letter and ladder, and writing and drawing.

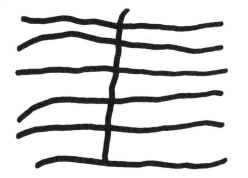

Not all discoveries lead to orthodox print

Follow this thought sequence carefully. Draw the examples.

Phillip made an 'L' that he called an 'L' and a '7'. Then he made an 'E' out of it. 'Look what else I made,' he said. After a pause, he continued, 'I can't think what else I could make of it.' His mother showed him how he could make it into a 'B'. Then Phillip drew a vertical line down the middle of the letter and said, 'Look what else I can make, a window.'

Then he wrote an 'E' at the bottom of the page and said, 'This is the letter that "window" starts with.'

So not all discoveries line up with *our* notions of printed language!

Phillip wrote another 'E', dipped his brush back into the paint and converted all his work into three blobs of paint!

(Grinnell and Burris, 1983)

Tuhi Ngaheu, four years
He kotiro kei roto te waka — a girl in the boat

He whare tenei — this is a house

17

Writing that may or may not have a message

Pages of scribble and pages of symbols are ways of making long statements with the signs that the child knows. This continues for a long time.

Letters will make long statements because the child can use them over and over again. Repetitions extend the statement.

Words can make a statement and the child can list all the words he or she knows.

Much of this activity is merely the production of large amounts of writing. It is not intended as a message.

'A string of all the signs I know,' or Katherine's 'silly poem' written at kindergarten, or Steven's list of letters, give no sign that the child intended to record a message.

Steven

Katherine, three years four months

I followed Jill into the kitchen where she was preparing a Chinese meal. She showed me a cookbook and told me of her Chinese cooking class. Moving around the kitchen while we talked, I picked up a piece of yellow lined paper off a counter top. I asked Jill if it was for my collection. She looked at it and said, 'No, I don't know where that came from.' Steven walked into the kitchen and I asked him if he knew anything about the paper. He said, 'Sure, I just did it.' While we were talking, Steven was drawing letters. No one was watching him, and no one had seen him put the paper on the counter top — a perfect example of unnoticed momentary writing activities.   (Taylor, 1983)

3 'I want to record a message'

The message is in the print

Up until now the child has been doing interesting things with print. He or she has learned some ideas about letters and the drawing/writing distinction, and has some plans for arranging letters in orders. The child has learned to see differences between some letters, has mastered different movement patterns, knows that you can repeat signs, and may write all or part of someone's name, usually their own.

Now there is an important shift when it becomes obvious that the child knows that print transmits a message.

At four years nine months Alison entered kindergarten in Australia. A few weeks later she solemnly presented her mother with a page of writing (scribble streamer). 'That's good,' said her mother. 'Will you read it to me?' 'Don't be silly, mummy,' said Alison. 'You know how to read. But I'm only little. I can only write yet.' Jan Turnbill told that story.

Tasha

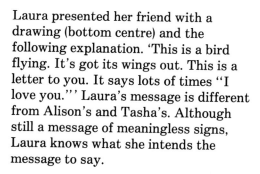

Laura, draws and scribbles

Alongside a scribble drawing Tasha invented some print, using different combinations of the letters she knew (top centre). She took it to her mother and said, 'What does it say?' She knew that she did not know what it said, but she was confident that her mother would know. Her mother responded to this trust and replied, 'Sahspno.' Tasha said 'Oh,' and returned to draw some more. The fact that Tasha asked for her message to be read confirmed that she believed messages can be put into writing.

Laura presented her friend with a drawing (bottom centre) and the following explanation. 'This is a bird flying. It's got its wings out. This is a letter to you. It says lots of times "I love you."' Laura's message is different from Alison's and Tasha's. Although still a message of meaningless signs, Laura knows what she intends the message to say.

Messages require words

'If my name is Jenny and my brother's name is Alan, and I have three dolls which have different names, and I am only four and haven't yet learned to write any words, perhaps I could make some names for my dolls. Make them in writing, that is, because they have names. Their names are Katrina, Sleepy-eye doll, and Debbie. I can use the signs I know, and I can copy some from books, I can use the same ones twice, and I can turn some around.

Now, each doll has a different name so each name-word must be different. If I have to use the same letters (there aren't many letters are there?) I could put them in different patterns.'

We do not know if that was what Jenny said to herself. All we know is that she brought three invented names made from real letters to her mother and said, 'That says Sleepy-eye doll, that says Katrina, and that says Debbie.'

Jenny knows some of the rules for writing words. She has made a start.

Tonn,4i

AUUDO

Jooi2

Jenny, four years eleven months

MiVMA   sapo (toad)

MiMiT   pato (duck)

OriM   oso (bear)

OgTMr   conejo (rabbit)

Martin, five years

MS NOJ Iso MS N 5NQ Os8o uS
QYw CñMe C Mco9ot 9o
                              NS

Francis (Maori boy), five years — 'my name!'

Emilia Ferreiro studied Spanish-speaking children in Mexico. She gives a fascinating example of a child's response at the same stage as Jenny. The child invented a word for cat (which would be gato in Spanish).

A O i

Then she invented a different word for the little cat (gatito).

O i A

Finally, struggling with the idea of three little cats she wrote

OAiOAiOAI

saying, 'One litle cat, the little cats here, another cat.' This example and the one that follows are discussed by Emilia Ferreiro and Ann Teberosky.

Martin was a Spanish-speaking child. He could print his name in capital letters and knew a few other letters. He made a list of animal names and

- each name was different
- he used the letter he knew
- a word had four or five letters.

He also wrote a sentence about this time in which each letter stood for a word.

M i L T E
Mi nena toma sol
(My little girl sits in the sun.)

Thrifty, conservative, using their own rules

Jamie

The signs at the top of this page are what Jamie wrote for his name and the ones at the bottom of the page are what Laura wrote for her name. Children make a few symbols go a long way, and the small number of signs is expanded rather slowly.

When they make a change they tend only to vary one thing at a time. They do not often step outside what they know and create totally new forms.

Like Martin (page 20) they seem to develop plans or rules for making forms and while they may not use our rules they systematically relate parts to one another.

Own names are important words

Most children begin to learn the letters of their own name which becomes their first word written in full.

But not always. Denise wrote her father's name 'John' before she wrote her own (see page 13).

Names go through stages of development. For many months Jenny signed herself as

Jehhy

and would not change.

Kelly, four years eleven months, practises her own name

In the next section Sally-Ann's development over six months shows what a learning resource her name was.

Laura

4 We follow Sally-Ann's progress

Out of the names of preschoolers . . .

Let us follow Sally-Ann over six months of her preschool life. She was three years four months when this record begins and I have selected only a few examples from her many pieces of work. Her interest in print is exceptional, spurred on perhaps by having two older sisters who go to school, and a father who does writing work at home. Her parents let her lead and respond to her requests. What she

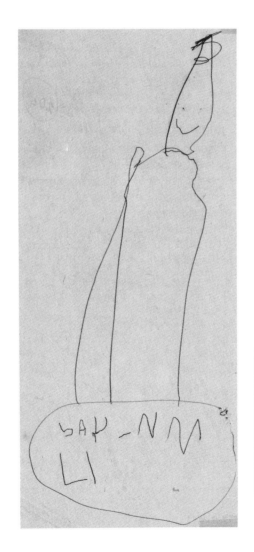

does with print is in some ways typical of preschool children who show an interest in writing. On the other hand she does things that are peculiar to her and rare in most children. For example she learns to take dictated spelling. This is useful. There are four people in her house who might spell words for her to write. Most children prefer a written copy of a word they do not know.

Comment

She uses blue pen on fawn paper.

Sally-Ann draws a person and signs her name (which is not an easy one to master).

The hyphen seems to have the status of a letter. Follow this in later examples.

The 'A' of ANN has been missed out.

The letters for SALLY are all there but their order or sequence is not yet important.

Diary

14 February

Sally-Ann made three Valentine cards. She signed one:

SALLY

The second one combined letters and mock writing.

The third one was more exploratory.

S   A
U   F

She said, 'That's an "F" but it's got an extra bit. I like doing "F"'s like that!'

Comment

Black pen, and pink chalk on white paper hearts.

Sally-Ann's writing shows several important achievements.

- She can write one real word keeping to the 'proper' forms.
- She explores pencil on paper and invents new forms.
- She 'knows' what a real 'F' looks like but she thinks it is fun to change it a little.

What she probably doesn't know yet is how close to an 'E' she has come.

Diary

Early March

This is my first example of her full name. The decoration seems to be an important part of the production.

Comment

Comment

Shiny, white paper; pink, purple, and yellow felt pens.

There is only one further item to be controlled for a perfect signature — one 'N' is reversed.

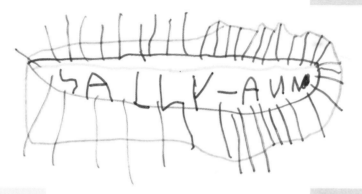

Late March

This is best called 'variations on a full name'.

Blue felt pen on lined paper. The lines are not ignored. Some attempt is made to use them.

SALLY-ANN

is extended by 'S's in front and 'N's at the end to fill up the line in the centre. The rest is variations on the letters in a name to fill up the framed space.

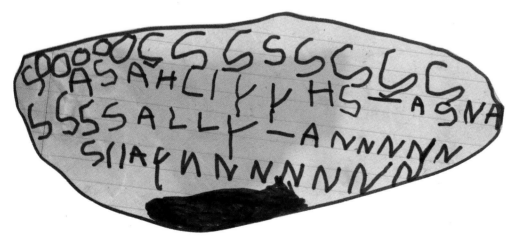

9 April

Her mother had no explanation for the appearance of this second real word 'hot'.

Red pen on an old greeting card.
   Sally-Ann could write little more than her name. Yet she wrote

YA   YAI   YAH   YAHL

and after each addition she asked her father to say what she had written. It is not surprising that she quickly learns a new word.

HOT

This extends her concept of a word. What *is* surprising is that it contains two new letters. However, they are easy ones to write.

10 April

Sally-Ann was playing with words. She wanted to spell something. She wrote

SA/LL

and asked, 'What does this say, Mummy?' Her mother said, 'Sall.' Sally-Ann was pleased. She replied, 'You use it in shop,' linking SALL and SELL.

Pencil, black felt pen on notepaper.
   Sally-Ann varies her signature.

SA/LL — A

Notice that she asked her mother what *part* of the word said. Also she linked the answer to a word she already knew.

Diary

29 April

First Sally-Ann wrote

        ST P

and then she added the 'O'.

        STOP

Trying something new she wrote

        ST H

and asked, 'What does that say, Daddy?' Then she asked for

        SHOP

and it was spelled out for her letter by letter.

Comment

Red felt pen on note pad.

    From our record so far we know that

        S H T O

are not new letters.

        P

is not covered in our examples but it is the first letter of the family name.

    Does

        STOP

come from some family experience like reading road signs? Or is she trying to get to SHOP and has she somehow linked together the sounds of those words?

    Notice that Sally-Ann is able to take a kind of dictation, when familiar letters are spelled for her. This is unusual in my experience. She does not need a visual model. Another child would.

    Sally-Ann already knows that letters have names, that is, each letter has some equivalent sound which you can say.

Diary

13 May

Sometimes writing is just practising what you already know.

Comment

Blue pen on note pad.

This repetition reminds me of how often Sally-Ann must have written the letters that make up her name.

14 May

This is repetition and practice of something new. Is it

        G   or   e (upside down)?

Notice the letter

                Ṡ

Is that a signature?

Blue felt pen on the back of a notice.

When we cannot watch the child at work we lose a lot of information. We guess about how it was done and we can often be quite wrong.

27

Diary

15 May

Sally-Ann writes

GO

in sequence seven times!

Comment

Green felt pen on lined paper.

A new word repeated seven times *and* a return to scribble.

Yesterday's letter was probably

G and not   e.

Has the emergence of

GO

got anything to do with a contrast with

STOP

which she wrote earlier?

Perhaps not! It is just as likely that this was about the time that Grandma came to stay.

Or, on the other hand, 'GO' may have been entirely accidental.

Diary

30 May

The picture is given a name using part of Sally-Ann's name. She said, pointing to it, that it was 'the picture's name'.

Comment

Black felt pen on lined paper.

The concept of 'a name' is clear to her. It can be recorded in print.

The hyphen does seem to be seen as a letter, and she is able to take a part of her name and use it as a new name for her drawing.

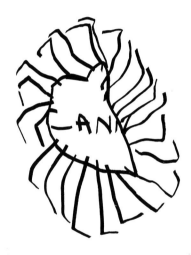

Early June

A signed drawing. The signature has been varied.

SHLYiANNe

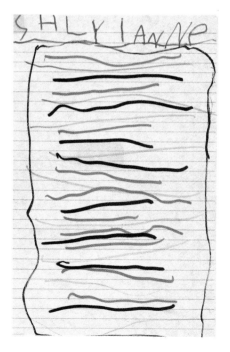

Felt pens — red, green and black on lined paper.

She can write her name and this signature is probably playful exploration.

Notice that

A   becomes   H
—   becomes   i
       or
Lly   becomes   LYi.

This is the first use of 'e' that I have seen in her record.

Diary

5 June

Here are all the letters that Sally-Ann knows, and there are some new ones.

I L H F E T T ℄
O P B 8
S 5

Watch the 'different T' (or is it a reversed 'J'?) We cannot tell what she is 'seeing' but we can watch how and when it changes.

SENTENCE CUBE

30

Diary

11 June

The family had just bought some goldfish. Sally-Ann drew two and began to write about them.

D H ʈ T

Then she checked with a parent on how to write

SEE
FISH

added   ʈ ʈ

and her signature.

14 June

Just a drawing. An important return to a different activity.

Diary

16 June

Back to a stick-letter theme, with variations and repetitions of

E   and   L.

Comment

Black pen on the back of a notice.

A simple, controlled comparison of how 'E' and 'L' are alike and different. This renewed attention to letters turns out to be important in the next month.

17 June

A long string of things she knows.

Then, inside the circles, she writes letters and says, 'Jokes for you, Daddy.'

'T' is still different from ⊥.

Blue felt pen on lined paper, lines ignored.

At the top of the page she writes a list of the letters she can remember.

In the circles she has written a special kind of message, a joke. She probably hopes that Daddy will be able to read the message and knows that she cannot.

Diary

26 June

Back to 'real' words and copying. I do not know why 'sea snake' was chosen but Sally-Ann practises this new word.

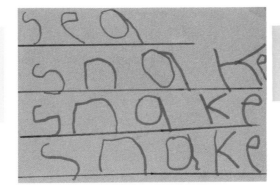

Comment

Green felt pen on green paper. She may have asked for lines to be ruled for her in this example.

29 June

More letters with the new ones

R   W   M

and the hyphen.

Blue felt pen on lined paper.

What other preschooler would be using a hyphen among her letters at this stage? Probably only one who had a hyphen in her name.

Diary

30 June

A list of 'all the letters I know' which suddenly changes in the last two lines to an alphabet!

In the sixth box from the top down the left-hand side we can see

+ + B

then to the right

A E F

and away she goes

H i ꞁ K L M N O P
Q R S T U V W

This is the first time I have seen

Q a K V W

in her work.

And now the 'ꞁ' is alphabetically in place and we can be sure that Sally-Ann has been making a distinction between

T and J

for some time. Only the direction of the hook has to be sorted out.

Comment

Green pen on green paper, with red felt pen outlines.

Most of the capital forms of letters have been practised. The only clearly lower-case letters before this have been 'e' and 'i'.

From a source such as a book, or a sister, or a parent, suddenly Sally-Ann has put her letter knowledge into a new arrangement. The order is not on likeness,

L E F

nor set by a spelling pattern as in the 'name'

— ANN

but it is a list of things you say. It is a system for collecting all the letters together: an alphabet.

This works for Sally-Ann because she has already discovered most of the letters. Note that the alphabet is a way of getting hold of the whole system, of tidying it up. But it is not the way Sally-Ann learned about letters.

Diary

4 July

Real words

SAL
STOP
GO
HOT
Si (is)

and invented words.

VW
AL
iP

6 July

Real messages can be written. Sally-Ann probably liked the message when someone spoke it. It was worth writing down. So the words were spelled for her, letter by letter:

NONSENSE. YOU ARE NOT GOING DIRTY.

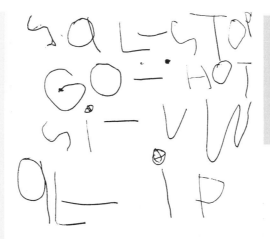

Comment

Red pen on note paper.
   Further confirmation of the concepts noted on 1 July.
   The construction of words is being explored.
   Now the hyphen is possibly being used to divide one word from another.

Another way of producing messages — ask your parent how to write the message. Because Sally-Ann can write words which are spelt for her letter by letter she could record this message. This is a hard way of writing unless you know a lot of letters.

Diary

1 July

Sally-Ann continues to explore. She breaks up the letters in her name with vertical lines.

Comment

A colourful sequence — red, yellow, purple, black and green. Felt pen on green paper.

Back to the known 'SALLY' with a slight change. Capital 'A' is now lower-case 'a'.

SaLLY

Strong purple lines divide the name into its letters. Quite clearly she understands that there are letters, and they make up names.

Brown felt pen on yellow paper.

This looks like an exploration of the idea that letters make word patterns.

3 July

And so to the invention of pretend words:

i H — L K

T V — Y +

complete with hyphens.

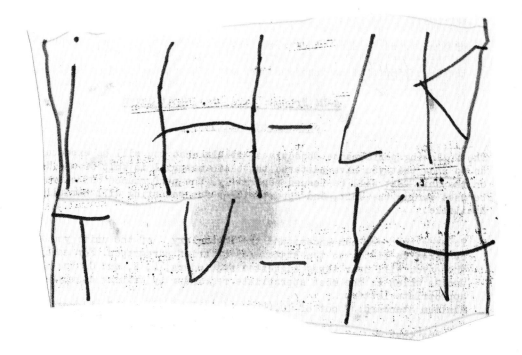

36

Diary

20 July

Copying from a model, Sally-Ann writes

Daddy

with lower-case 'd's and then on a different sheet she writes

SaLLY

Daddy.

Comment

Pencil on yellow paper.

She copies from a model and adds to her control of lower-case letters.

It was a happy coincidence that 'Sally' and 'Daddy' both have

a and y

and they also both have a doubled letter:

LL and dd.

It is experiences like this, chance happenings, that give children a sense that there is a system in there somewhere.

22 July

This is the beginning of story-writing. What a long way she has come in the last six months. Sally-Ann could be six, or five or four. She is really only three years and ten months. On one side of her paper she had drawn a picture with an odd-looking tree in it. She made up her story, asked for the spelling to be dictated, and asked for 'h' to be written down so she could copy it.

Blue felt pen on top of a typed and xeroxed sheet which is ignored.

In this example we see that Sally-Ann had the language and the urge to write. She composed the message, got help, could take dictation, knew when she needed to copy *and* she has made a great advance in the use of lower-case letters.

For her last story in this series go back to page 5.

Diary

'Now she is five.'

Sally-Ann wrote the story about the 'wonky tree' 14 months before she began school. She had been at school for four weeks when she produced this story.

Independence has been achieved. She constructs her messages in her own words and records the sounds that she can hear in those words. We did not capture the transition.

I I ma
SIt Be
Cos
I Ho nr

BoD to
Play wev
Said Me
Sid Sally

'I am sad because I have nobody to play with, said me, said Sally'

And after another six weeks Sally-Ann recorded her enjoyment of the Santa Claus parade.

We went to the Santa parade and saw Father Christmas and we got a flag too. The flag had write on it. It said, 'After the Santa parade take me home and colour me in or put me in a tidy bin.' I coloured him in. Father Christmas was smiling on the flag. It was fun and then we went home.

We went to the Santa pared and saw farthe cesmar and We got a fage too. the fage had write on it

it said afeba the Santa partd tard me home and calr me in or put me in a terd ben I calvd him in . farthe cesmar was smiling on the fage it was fan and thev we went home

Sally-Ann, five years two months, after ten weeks at school.

5 Individual differences at school entry

Drawing

On the left are six responses to 'draw a man' requests. They suggest that past opportunities have resulted in quite different kinds of practising and exploring.

We can compare how children's drawing changes once they come to school, still without any formal instruction in how to draw a man or a woman.

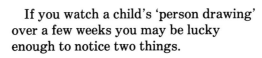

If you watch a child's 'person drawing' over a few weeks you may be lucky enough to notice two things.

Secondly, although the plan is similar for drawings done several weeks apart the programme changes and becomes more complex.

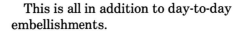

Firstly, the child tends to have a plan or scheme for producing the drawing. He runs through the same programme of movements and produces big and little versions of the same model.

This is all in addition to day-to-day embellishments.

The pairs of drawings on the right show the changes in the drawings of three children between five years and five years six months.

Writing

All these children are five years old.
They have just entered school and they
are at different stages of writing
development.

Angela

Angela
iS Look
Iam B
MoTherup

Christine

Leah

To Barbara i
in the holidayS
Went to the farm.
and rolled in the
hay.and Went to feed
the pig Swith Grandma.
and go to get the
Cows With Toto.

Love Krom
Leah.

Important messages

An untutored child, aged five years and not yet at school, left this message for his mother, Glenda Bissex.

Punctuation

Ann Henshaw set out to find what five-year-olds knew about full stops. Here are some of the very different answers she got to her question, 'Tell me about these dots. Why do you think we have them?'

'Some words need them — some words don't.'

'Dad's going to tell me when we go in the caravan.'

'It's at the end of the page so you don't go off.' (She pointed to the end of the line.)

'It stops you from doing writing.'

'It's at the end of your work you put one. (Chuckle) You get told off if you don't'.

'It's to finish a sentence. If you don't put a full stop and you write a letter people might think you've forgotten to post the other half.'

A reminder note

A five-year-old brother said to his sister, 'You can have some of my french fries.' She responded with more enthusiasm than he expected, and here is his spontaneous drawing of the incident. Perhaps this is like making a mental note of something we want to remember. Jacqueline Goodnow reported this in her book about early drawing behaviour.

6 How can a parent help?

What should I correct?

Not much. Until children can see a distinction for themselves you will find it very hard to change their ways. And when they can see it they will probably change before you can think of how to teach it.

For some of the funny things that children do, there are some explanations. We could look at some of these.

A child who is given a lot of print to copy may start anywhere. He or she may go down instead of across or start at the bottom and go to the top. Halfway up they may wander off in another direction. That way they may easily omit some of the letters.

Children have more control over their own development in writing if they are working mostly on things they know (as Sally-Ann did). They are learning most when they are constructing letters and words rather than copying them.

'But how do they learn new words?' you might ask. Like learning to speak, children seem to make new words out of what they already know. It is a kind of grafting process. If the discoveries are useful they live on: the ones that don't work disappear.

Children are very flexible. They may begin at the right side of a page and write easily from right to left, reversing all the letters. If you give them a starting sign on the left they will probably follow the rules of English writing and go from left to right. Many languages are written in different directions, so I suppose it is useful that children are flexible. They can then adapt to their English or Hebrew or other scripts.

For English there are three directional principles to be learned: go left to right; move top to bottom; and return quickly from right to left and start again.

These rules have to be learned as ways of placing yourself in space. I think blank pages help the child with this learning, and rules and lined pages make the task harder. Once the child controls the spaces in which he or she writes then the child can begin to use the lines. Lines call for greater control over movements but they also interfere with judgements about direction and spaces.

(Graves, 1979)

Because of all these things to be learned, children write all over paper in peculiar ways and they turn letters upside down and back to front.

Sometimes these changes are not noticed. They could be accidental. They could be an experiment, to see what happens. They could be a deliberate way of trying to find another letter form.

I think we should be relaxed about the preschooler's exploration of letter and word forms. Control will come as more writing forms are mastered.

One author reports:

Cynthia writes all the numbers she knows, once in the conventional way, and again reversing the right-left or up-down relationships.

Jacqueline Goodnow found that children show space problems in drawing, also. How do you add two more wheels to a train, when two wheels have pre-empted the space?

And just because you have well-established habits and have lost your flexibility with age, do not interpret this example as a mess until you have turned the page slowly through 360 degrees to see what you are able to read.

How should a parent respond to this effort? 'Tell me about it,' would be a good start. The story you get may not be the one the teacher got, but it will probably be about clowns.

'And what did you write?' would be a useful follow-up question. My guess is that this child would point unsystematically at her own attempts at letters. She wrote because the teacher wrote. The idea of copying the teacher's letters has not yet occurred to her. That's OK.

Setting the tone for writing

The child leads, the adult follows. This means that we must take our cues from the children themselves.

Laura, at four and a half, said she was doing her homework. (She had three brothers at school.) She filled in the squares in her colouring book with signs that were nothing in particular. She did not seem to be very advanced in writing.

As she worked she was chanting the sing-able version of the alphabet. There is no evidence of how she matched the song to the writing but why did she add one extra square? Well, she ended up on the last line with the words, 'Now tell me what you think of me.' If you try to match that, word-for-square, you will find that you are one square short. So Laura drew one in!

Laura was writing, saying the alphabet, and doing the kind of word-by-word matching that can be useful in early reading.

Like Laura, the child should be free to start, to lead, and to work independently. Exploring with a pencil does NOT mean that adults should take no notice or adopt a hands-off policy. An available adult can come in very handy.

- Give your attention to the child's work.
- Supply information asked for.
- 'Read' the message if requested.
- Tutor, when asked to by the child.
- Offer help, but don't be pushy.

On the other hand, if you ignore what children are trying to write they will do less and less of it.

If you know your child well, and you leave the doors open for exploring to take place, you will often know how to support your child's next discoveries.

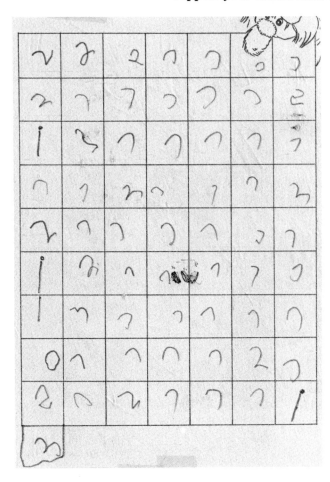

46

Should one teach children their letters?

If you were to ask me whether I would rather teach a Sally-Ann who discovered most of the alphabet (and knows which letters are like which others and how they differ), or Peter who has been taught to say his alphabet and to recognise all his letters, I am sure I would find Sally-Ann easier to teach.

She knows

• how to work things out for herself
• when to seek my help
• the construction of letters and which bits added to what make new letters.

She happens to know the letter names and I consider that a bonus, but not essential for the way I would teach in school.

If, however, a teacher or school assumes that children must know their letters before they come to school, what Peter had been taught would be important.

My point is that the child who discovers all these things about print through exploring writing knows *more* than a child who is simply taught his or her letters.

When a child explores print he or she is exploring the system and its rules. As the child plays with

h   n   r   u

or struggles with the distinctions between

L   E   I   l   F

or the seemingly different group like

Y   K   V   A   W   X   y   k

one suspects that the child is struggling with the critical differences between letters. The horizontal bars in the second group of letters or the angles in the third group may be the learning that the child is struggling with.

There is a fair chance that the child's own approach to these features (which are hard to talk about) is probably a quicker route to control of the forms than having to learn 52 letters by copying and repeated practice.

If you think about it, the differences between

h   n   r   u

are the differences that we retain no matter what size type or type of print we use. They *are* the critical differences, and that is what the preschooler who discovers print is working out for him or herself.

Look back at Sally-Ann's record and review what she was learning about the relationships

• of one letter to another
• of letters to words
• of words to messages
• and of letters and words to stories.

She knew her letters and the many varied relationships in which they occur in printed messages.

Letters are only important because they make a difference to the messages we get from them.

In this example Andrew is just beginning this exploration of the letters we use in English.

When Andrew was in his fourth year, he became noticeably interested in the alphabet. A set of plastic letters was kept in the television room. Andrew occasionally used them to form his name, but for the most part he had unconventional ways of playing with them. Nina spoke of his 'making his own letters' by turning the plastic letters around to form new shapes. Nina described how Andrew used the 'I' and the 'C' to make 'D', and how he took two 'C's to make 'S'. She explained that he would make a new letter and then come up to her and ask, 'What letter does that look like?' Nina would then join in the game. Denny Taylor describes this in her book, *Family Literacy*.

Can't I save my child some of the struggle?

Not really. Children will change their view of the world when they discover some mismatch. Although the problem looks simple to you, it is usually more complex from where they are.

Telling may have little effect. Demonstrating is a little better, especially if you go away and leave the model with a child. Eight weeks later the child may have put it all together.

Some child psychologists have suggested that children learn and change their view of things when they can see two things in conflict — things that ought to look the same don't.

Children often get a set idea about print. They seem to form strange ideas. They may cling to these ideas even when we give them examples to prove them wrong. For several weeks or months they continue to do it their way because that way makes sense for the present.

Then one day they are surprised to see their way of writing is really different from someone else's way. They see the difference for themselves and have two options. They can stay with their old way, or they can adjust their whole system of ideas to include the new example. It may take several encounters before children suddenly do it in a more acceptable way. Gradually children will reconstruct the English writing system, making it their own.

'RUDF '

When five-year-old Paul wrote this, I was reading outside on the deck and he was in the house. After several unsuccessful attempts to talk with me, he took rubber letter stamps from his set, printed this message, and delivered it to me with feeling. Do you know what it says? 'Are you deaf?' Of course, I put down my book. He had broken through print with print.

A month after printing 'RUDF,' Paul types 'EFUKANOPNKAZIWILGEVUAKANOPENR.' You are probably having as much difficulty as I did deciphering it. Paul read it for me: 'If you can open cans, I will give you a can opener.' I mentioned to him that most people, when they write, leave a space between words. A few minutes later he typed 'EFU WAUTH KLOZ IWEL GEVUA WAUTHENMATHEN' (If you wash clothes, I will give you a washing machine). Soon he was separating all his words. When he wrote by hand, which he did more often than typing, he segmented with dots rather than spaces. For a time he carried this strategy so far that he segmented some affixes as well: 'PAUL.IS.GOWING .TO.RUN.A.RAWND.AND. JUMP. AND.EXRSIZ.' He titled this 'RE.PORT. KARD.ON.SPORTS.' Dots were Paul's reinvention of a device used in ancient manuscripts; in fact in the very earliest manuscripts words were not separated at all. So Paul was recapitulating a bit of the history of writing.

In the evolution of his spelling of the word *directions*, we can see Paul's ability to make finer and more complex distinctions:

5:7 DRAKTHENS (five years seven months)
5:8 DRAKSHINS (five years eight months)
7:5 DIRECKSHONS (seven years five months)
7:5 DIREKSHONS (seven years five months)
8:1 DIRECTIONS? (unsure whether it was -TION or -TOIN) (eight years one month)
8:4 DIRECTIONS (eight years four months)

Clearly *he* regarded his spelling as perfectible rather than as fixed word patterns to be repeated from memory.

Paul wrote a great deal before first grade — and even before he was able to read much. His use of invented spellings enabled him to write freely from the start in what may seem a surprising variety of compositional forms: signs, labels and captions; stories; little books; directions; lists or catalogues; newspapers; notes, letters and greeting cards; statements; and school-type exercises. *He wrote spontaneously in more different forms than he used in school assignments.*

Patterns of Development in Writing: A Case Study
Glenda L. Bissex

Shouldn't children spell correctly?

Yes. And no!

I wonder whether any spelling programme could have taken Sally-Ann through as much as she taught herself in the six months between three years four months and three years ten months. She cannot yet spell many words but she has a sound foundation and a rather well-tuned sense that there are right and wrong ways of writing words. And yet she will play with letter forms and spelling patterns just to learn more about how they all work together.

How do you prepare a very important letter to someone? Probably your first concern is to get the ideas down, and the spelling and punctuation get little attention. On rereading your own draft you discover that the message needs to be altered to read more clearly. Then you might tidy up the technical detail of spelling and punctuation and ask someone else to read it. It would be irritating but almost inevitable that the second reader misunderstood one or two points.

Further editing is needed before the important letter is in its final form, having gone through several drafts. (If you are a person who has a secretary, you may avoid some of these because you can rely upon a secretary's skills.)

So it is with children. When they come to express themselves the essential aspects of their writing are the ideas and messages. Matters of spelling,

Katy's sample shows writing vocabulary of eight correct words but notice how close she is to 'up' (qu) 'little' (ttlie) 'David' (Dvid) 'car' (cr) 'on' (og) and 'here' (the). (The only non-helpful responses are 'g' and 'th' for 'is'.)

punctuation, neatness, correctness, and grammar are not the first things we should foster. While we are insisting on accuracy we are probably killing off the inspiration to write. And if you do not write you do not practise, and you do not learn to write accurately anyway.

Today older children are encouraged to produce drafts which they edit in various ways.

I believe that there should be room for new discoveries, and that the things already learned should be produced accurately. Exploration changes to accuracy as new things come under the child's control.

The child who is always accurate may be a child who is afraid to venture into new experiences. I would rather have a venturesome child who tries new things, and makes discoveries along the way of what works and what does not work, than a child who produces unexciting but precise work.

You might ask how I can justify this. I know that the former child will continue to teach himself new things long after I have ceased to be his teacher.

What can I do?

- You can increase opportunities, and give support and encouragement so that the child feels that 'I can play around with writing.'

- You can make the child feel that 'When I write other people are interested in it.'

- You can signal to children that your first interest is in their meaning, and what they intended to write. (They will not trust themselves to explore if you are always ready to correct them.)

- If you teach children to write by copying they may come to believe that writing is only possible when there is a model to copy. This will block off discoveries.

- A learner who always works from a model is not, usually, an active learner. An active learner compares, sees possibilities, changes his or her thinking, and makes interesting connections. Writers need to be active learners.

With writing in mind

Adrian was nearly six, and he was an active learner. Here is his conversation with his teacher.

A: I'm not going to write a story today.
T: Why not?
A: Because I want to read.
T: But you write good stories and you learn to write lots of words.
A: I can *write* all the words.
T: OK, you tell me all the words.
A: I am going to the shops with my mother and Silia is coming too and my mother works in a factory (pause) fac-tor-y (pause) and my father works in a bar. He gets lots of money for (pause) . . . .
T: How do you write 'lots'?
A: It's like 'got'. And Silia is coming to school soon.
T: How do you write 'soon'?
A: It's got two 'O's.
T: Can you write it?
A: (Writes) It's like 'moon'.
T: How do you know 'moon'?
A: It's like 'zoo'.

How can I help?

Have your child work alongside you when you are writing — letters, shopping lists, filling out forms, or when siblings are being helped with their homework. Talk to your child about the writing you are doing.

Point out writing at the shops, in the advertising that arrives in your letterbox, on the road signs, or at your child's favourite fastfood shop, and talk about this print.

Encourage children to add their 'bit', whatever stage they are at, to the letters you write to relatives. If the relative puts in a 'kiddy message' in the reply, don't just read it to the child. Show the child the message.

When you leave messages for the family, perhaps with magnetic letters on the fridge door, let your preschooler help you make them.

There will come a time when you can leave a little written message for the child. After that opportunities will come thick and fast.

7 The child at school

Will my child be ready for school?

There are many schools which expect very little of children in writing. Somehow they think of this as something to be learned in school. And in some ways this has been true.

Mathew, five years one month, on his second day at school
Read from the bottom up:

- signature
- my family
- letters

A good start!

If parents believe that writing begins at school, then children do not learn to explore print at home, and they arrive at school knowing little. As schools have to teach large groups of children they tend to instruct, rather than to let children explore. Discovering print is a preschooler's luxury.

If you have shown an interest in your preschooler's attempts to write, the chances are he or she will be very well-prepared for any programme they will meet in school.

This was a kindergarten task.

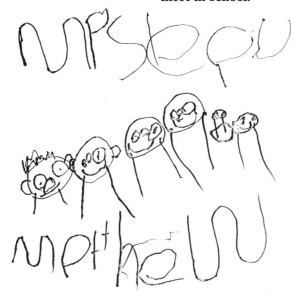

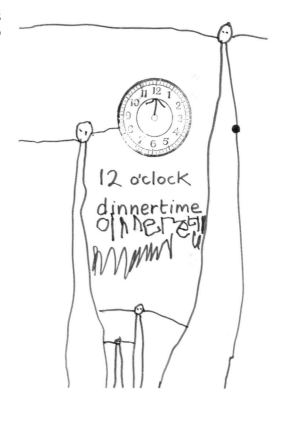

12 o'clock
dinnertime

What should I expect when my child goes to school?

There are so many different programmes that I find it difficult to answer this question. I will take three examples.

In some schools children's ability to form letters will be developed by workbook and handwriting lessons. Gradually all letters will be covered.

At the same time children will be learning letter names and sounds and some words needed in their reading. These will also be practised in workbook exercises.

The principle is *not* one of discovery but of somehow impressing the form of the word on the child by having him sound it, read it, and write it many times. This is strangely different from what the preschooler does naturally in discovering writing.

The examples on the right show how different children respond to a standard task.

On the same day in three different writing books *identical triplets* produced these samples. The first child traces the teacher's letters. The second child writes her own letters. The third child copies under the teacher's letters. These are different responses from identical children from the same home.

Being taught

Some people prescribe what little children need to learn, and design little tests.

The workbook task on letters (see below) is a sorting and matching task on the lower and upper-case alphabet. The question is, 'Has Johnny learned the pairs?'

The teacher-made copying task (see right) is intended to give practice in writing the words in the reading book. The questions are, 'Can Johnny get letters and spaces right when he copies?' and 'Will this help him to read his book?' Formal lessons for teaching children in Nursery School to write were bound to be published sooner or later. The question you should ask yourself is 'How well do these formal exercises link with what my child is trying to do?'

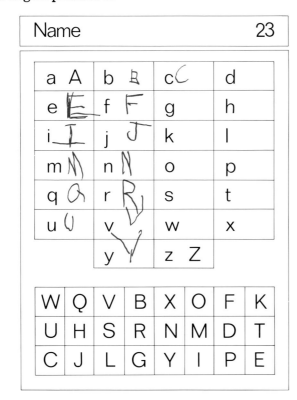

Name			23

a A	b ᗺ	c C	d
e E	f F	g	h
i I	j J	k	l
m M	n N	o	p
q Q	r R	s	t
u U	v V	w	x
	y Y	z Z	

W	Q	V	B	X	O	F	K
U	H	S	R	N	M	D	T
C	J	L	G	Y	I	P	E

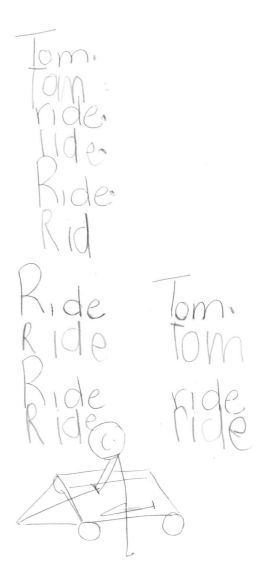

Allowing more scope for discovery

A second approach is to have the children draw pictures and dictate stories which the teacher writes.

Children may trace the teacher's story or copy underneath. Before long the children have learned to write some of the sentences or words or letters for themselves, and the teacher encourages this. The more the children write the bigger the vocabulary of words they can write becomes, until they have a good control over the little words that occur so often in English. They deserve help with the bigger words when they are working so well on composing stories and getting most of those little words correct.

Even with the bigger words the children begin to see how words work and they attempt parts of these for themselves. Most of this occurs before spelling lessons begin.

As words and composing come under control the child is free to write more creatively. We cannot push for this freeing-up too soon because the young writer may not feel in control of the task.

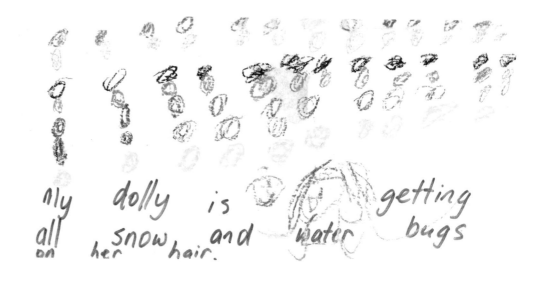

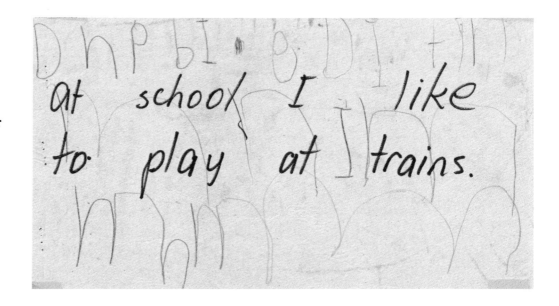

Somehow story-telling and story-reading experiences come together and you may begin to notice the style of a favourite author coming through.

Notice in Kay's story that she is not far removed from the stereotyped story that begins with a well-practised sentence starter. Yet you may detect something of the style of her favourite author whose books she is just becoming able to read for herself — Dr Seuss — and in particular *The Cat in the Hat*. So we get easy-to-write stories, based on her present control over sentence patterns and words, but composed with the lilt of a Seuss text.

In time this leads to the stories on the next page. In the second year at school these boys have made interesting drawings and stories which explain them.

here is a house
said Betty. Yes
said Paul. Yes
said Ben. I said
yes, too. Ben
said it is a blue
house. Yes said
Betty. Yes said
Paul I said yes two

Kay

I Would like to be a Engine driver and I would like to go And look at I Station at Australia because. I like Australs trains

Clinton

I Went to see a castle and I saw a swimming Pool and I Swam in The swimming Pool and I Went home

Frederick

Invented writing

A third approach to writing is to let children write, without worrying about whether the letters correspond in any way to words. The children invent their messages and then they invent the spelling. Only the children can reread the messages at first because they bear little correspondence to 'real' English. Gradually, as children meet words in their classroom and in their reading, some of the spellings become traditional and you will recognise them.

An important outcome of invented spelling can be this. Wanting to write a word, the children say the word slowly to themselves and try to find letters to write for the sounds they hear in the word to be written. They do a careful analysis of the sounds in the words, and from what they know about English words and letters they construct what they think the spelling will be. Children get very good at this. The teacher may do two things with a word that is not traditionally spelled. She may leave it as a good attempt, or she may show them how it could be changed slightly to make it 'real' English.

Being able to write words from this kind of analysis is a powerful strategy for getting the words you want in your composition down on paper. This is a constructive activity. The child engages in much word work, just as the preschooler does in discovering things about print.

A child's writing at the start of the programme, right, and after 12 weeks, below.

The frequently-used words gradually come into correct form and a writing vocabulary builds up. More and more control is gained over accurate performance as the systems of printed language become known.

In invented spelling the child is using a knowledge of spoken language, and is asking him or herself, 'What do I hear in the word I'm trying to write?'

Having isolated some sound or sound pattern the child is then saying, 'What do I know about writing that sound?'

Researchers found preschoolers who became very good at this way of writing. They found that a particular child would develop consistent ways of recording some sounds in English. They also found that different children would adopt the same non-English ways of spelling.

Children who already knew most of the alphabet seemed to be using it as a guide to finding letters.

BOT   KAM   Yl   (while)

Vowels were often omitted and this is because they are harder to hear than the consonants.

MN   DG   GRL

If you are using the alphabet names as a guide and you want to write the word 'chick' you would go searching what you know — ABCDEFGH — H — H . . . and you would record the first sound in 'chick' as H. Of course creative children will not be limited to a single approach, although they may be limited by the way they pronounce the words.

Pim was a Thai child growing up in the USA. She went to an English-speaking preschool. Her bilingual parents shared her children's books with her in either Thai or English. Pim started invented spelling of English when she was four years three months.

By the time she was five years two months her reading of English was very accurate and in advance of her invented writing in English.

It is my guess that what Pim is doing here is adding to English script the little circles that are a feature of Thai script.
Age: Five years two months.

Then Pim returned to Thailand. She wrote a letter to her aunt when she was six years four months. The underlined words are her invented writing in Thai. Having returned to Thailand she put to use what she had learned about writing (in English) by learning to write and invent words in the Thai language and script.

Should we interfere with invented spelling?

Some researchers and some educators have said we should encourage more and more writing and that, in time, the invented spelling will shift to English spelling as the child learns more about written language.

There is a new opportunity, when the child begins to read, to notice the ways of English words and to compare them with one's own writing.

Fascinating examples of what children notice and how they build these into their stories can be found. One child drew blanks between words like this:

I ☐ going ☐ with ☐ Dad

while yet another used underlining:

Iamgoingwith Dad.

Both were trying to record the breaks or spaces between words.

For some children being allowed to write only the sounds they can hear produces a long statement that may be difficult to read.

Only when I can recognise what has happened in the cat story (on the right), am I ready to help this girl develop from this point. She hears the first letters of words and can record them accurately. I would not want to make her self-conscious about what she has left out nor feel that she ought to write full words. What I can do easily is help that child to hear the last letters in words as a first step in further development.

(I happen to know that she would find that an easier task than to hear the second sound in a word. First and last sounds have silence around them just as first and last letters have spaces around them.)

It helps us to understand how early 'errors' get corrected, and how we can understand un-English spellings as exciting explorations made by children into the spelling system, if we look at the invented spellings produced by some young and some older children.

Invented spelling can lead to a control over writing that frees the child to write the messages he wants to write. Otherwise he may only ever write the stilted messages that are made up of the words he already knows.

Go back to Sally-Ann's case study and re-read her first story written independently after she went to school (p.38).

MKesNs

TrLr&Ls

IMN

ILMC

My cat is nice.
Turtles are slow.
I am nice.
I like my cat.

From *Language Stories and Literacy Lessons* by Jerry Harste, Carolyn Burke and Virginia Woodward.

A message that has to be shared

This is a spontaneous writing task, reporting a big event by letter to a friend, Mrs Sexton. The letter is about another friend, 'the bala ec-samena' (the ballet examiner).

Do you need a translation?
Dear Mrs Sexton,
My tooth has fallen out. I was very happy and I had another wiggly tooth and Daddy pulled it out last night.
    And did you know that I was the only one in the whole of the ballet class to get Honours out of the three, and of the whole of Wanganui (the town).
    And would you like a copy of my certificate?
Love from
Emma

Dear Mrs. Sexton 🖊 my tooth has folen awt I was very Happy and I Had a nothoe wegale tooth and daddy puold it awt larst nit and did you know wat I was the onle one in the howl bala clas to get Hones awt ov the three of the howl of Waganui and wod you lik a cope of my setefcewt ? . ✶✶✶ Love from Emma.

Which way of learning is best?

So which way of learning to write is best? Each has its good and bad points:

- Stories may have little place in the workbook programme, for letters and words must be learned.

- Letter and word learning must be monitored in the story-writing programme because for some children their control grows slowly.

- Accuracy must accumulate in the invented spelling programme or else the child will habituate invented forms of common words.

The real answer is that all programmes have to be monitored to ensure progress for individual children, especially children who do not find learning easy.

Any method may help — or hinder. It creates opportunities to learn but it does not create the learning. It is the children who do that through their own activity.

Dear Nanny,
I wish you a Merry Christmas and a Happy New Year.
I am at school now and I like it very much.
I send you a calender made by myself.

Many Greatings from Manuka

8 Let your child lead

What is good preschool progress?

- If your child goes to school knowing some letters, a few words, and enjoys writing, that is good preparation.

- Your child may write little messages or stories. That is excellent for a teacher to build on.

- Your child may play with words and letters, and that should make any of the programmes I described easier for him.

- Your child may have got to invented spelling by herself. Fine, she can build on that.

- What you may want to look out for is when your child has one set of skills and one set of ideas about what writing is, and the school has a programme with different demands. That may confuse your child *for a while*. Your support will see him or her through. What has to happen is that the child has to come to relate what he or she knows to the new programme. It will take a little time.

As with the preschooler, I suspect that the quickest way to get the match between what the child can do, and what the new school expects, is to let the child discover the similarities.

We need to watch carefully how children respond to the settings we put them in. To the young child, writing at home may seem to be different from writing at school.

I doubt whether there is a fixed sequence through which all children must pass. The path to progress is likely to be different for different children, since they come from diverse backgrounds and pay attention to the things around them in very individual ways.

Discoveries

It does seem important to value the discoveries that children make.

Mark, as he says, is five (centre page). He may be taking an inventory of the words he knows but follow through his sequences (moving vertically down the lists). There must be a hundred kinds of contrasts on this page — groupings by letter, by family, by meaning, by letter order likenesses and letter order contrasts, word families and 'far out' groups like 'doll', 'ball', 'bell', and 'I'll'.

Sandy (right side), a preschooler, was putting many things together. In her play she got ideas about adoption from a conversation she heard. She invented adoption papers, wrote them, costed the project, thought up a computer evaluation of the adoptive parents and wrote it out.

What interesting ways of bringing together what she knew!

Sandy

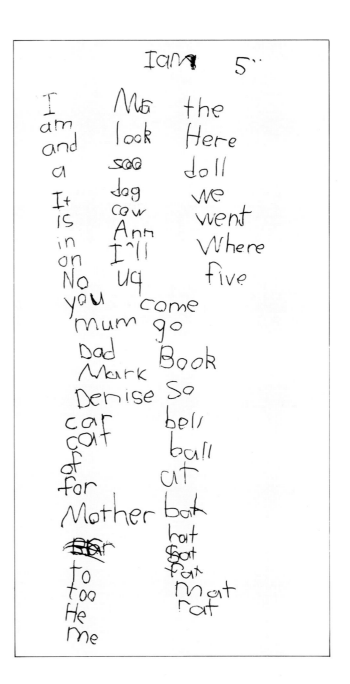

Control and freedom

There is a dilemma in helping children to arrive at good creative writing. The more control they have over writing letters, words, sentence patterns and story forms, the freer they are to be creative in their stories.

It is easy to conclude that if we teach children all about letters, make them learn some words and get the writing of correct sentences underway, then they will be free to write 'good' stories.

The dilemma is that most plans for teaching letters, words and correct sentence-writing give children strange ideas about what writing stories is about. They concentrate on getting it all correct and on forming their letters, becoming intent on this rather than on composing interesting stories.

Lessons can kill the child's interest in writing stories. We should retain the freedom and fun of writing stories at all costs.

Development and writing

We need to overcome our own concern that a child must always write correct English. We do not always speak correct English and we accept that a two-year-old will not speak correct English. A child will gradually learn more and more about what correct English is as he or she grows and continues to talk.

What happens if we adopt a similar kind of trust in learning to write? This would lead us to accept that the child will at first write:
• no real English words,
• then a word or two we recognise,
• then some words right and some words wrong,
• then most words right and a few words wrong.

We go on learning how to spell new words we have not had to spell before. We should expect child writers to write words they have not yet learnt to spell and to make some 'errors'.

What is my role as a parent?

So your role as a parent is to:

• provide opportunities for exploration
• provide materials
• be in touch with the child's attempts
• notice change when it occurs

and to marvel.

Most important of all, you need to be

• available
• attentive to your child's intention
• able to follow the child's line of enquiry
• able to supply help in his or her terms.

And you have to feel comfortable about letting the child lead.

When Steven was three years and six months of age, he sent a letter to his friend Andrew Simms. Steven sealed the envelope without showing his mother what he had written. He then asked her to address the envelope, and together they took the letter to the post office. When I asked Nina Simms about the letter that Andrew had received from Steven, she described his reaction. She said Andrew was really pleased to receive a letter, and when she had asked him if he understood what Steven had written, he had replied 'of course.' Nina could not find the letter, but she described it as a page of circles with lines through them. When Steven was four years and three months, he wrote Andrew another letter. This time he wrote his name four times on a piece of yellow lined paper, and once again, he posted it with his mother. Steven did not continue writing letters; however, he has been the recipient of letters from friends that have moved away from his neighborhood. Fifteen months after Steven wrote to Andrew, he has received a reply. Andrew (five years and six months) has sent a letter to Steven. He wrote 'Steven' and then 'Andrew' on a piece of paper; with Nina he put it in an envelope which she addressed, and together they took it to the post office.